In Praise of the Author

From Soil and Soul by Jenny Bates is a collection by a mystic, and a mystical spirit pervades its pages. Though many of the poems were inspired by Gustave Doré's engravings of New and Old Testament scenes, the poet dwells in a prelapsarian space. Divisions between human and animal, human and plant, are uncertain and dynamic, as seen in the poem "Fear": "You become the Deer/ You can do it." Well-known Biblical scenes and characters breathe and speak again in Bates' fervent imagination. In "Sign of the Cross," she declares, "I want the Christ dethroned / and sandaled // barefoot even better / who knows how the tip // of a wheat stalk feels." Jenny Bates speaks for the unseen and the uncanny; she knows how to "feel the assembling the / trembling of wings." To read *From Soil and Soul* is to feel unity with the natural and ancient worlds.

— Joan Barasovska, author of *Orange Tulips*
(Redhawk Publications, 2022)

From Soil and Soul starts off magnificently with "Unbroken Taper" and continues mining emotion, our relationship with God and nature at this same high level right through the end. The lines that held me breathless from the first were " I smell roses from nowhere, it is fifteen degrees outside." These lines define poets and poetry itself. Bates offers beauty, insights, springboards for deep thought, in each subsequent poem, where her words take us beyond ourselves, into the depths of our relationship with the earth and our own relationship with the Creator. Fittingly, after noting the end poems were inspired by an ancient illustrated Bible she ends with a prime that takes us on a meditation of the ancient Canonical Hours of the Forest, opening our hearts with her striking imagery to the way ahead for us. A brilliant collection.

— Joan Leotta, Poet, Author, Story Performer

From Soil and Soul: musings on the irredeemable spirit, invites us to join the poet on her journey- grounded in earth and aspiring for redemption; a communion with the divine through devotion to Mystery's manifestations in the natural world. In this work of ekphrastic poetry drawing inspiration from the 19th century artist, Gustave Doré's bible illustrations, Jenny dares to share her "irredeemable spirit"- a yearning for grace amidst despair where ancient texts inform a new and needed mythology. Jenny's poetry challenges the darkness with subtle word play and music, a quiet humor, the surprise of paradox and non-sequitur where the sensual and spiritual co-create the whole of the holy. And so this book of ancient stories told anew proves rich and rewarding. Indeed, enchanting. Jenny writes into being a world of passion and magic. Her poetry- a breath of prayer. Blessed be.

—Steve Braff, author of *Forty Days* (Cholla Needles Press), delights in reading, recording, writing, and teaching poetry

Also by the Author

Opening Doors: an equilog of poetry about Donkeys

Coyote With Coffee

Visitations

Slip

Where the Deer Sleep

Essential

From Soil and Soul:
musings on the irredeemable Spirit

Jenny Bates

Copyright © 2024 by Jenny Bates

All rights reserved. This book or parts thereof may not be reproduced in any form, stored in any retrieval system, or transmitted in any form by any means—electronic, mechanical, photocopy, recording, or otherwise—without prior written permission of the publisher, except as provided by United States of America copyright law. For permission requests, write to the publisher,

Redhawk Publications
The Catawba Valley Community College Press
2550 US Hwy 70 SE
Hickory NC 28602

ISBN: 978-1-959346-41-8
Library of Congress Number: 2024932344

Printed in the United States of America

Book and Cover Layout by Melanie Johnson Zimmermann

redhawkpublications.com

First Printing 2024

Raven with Branch cover photo by Steve Braff

Author's photo by Toni Lindahl

Special Thanks

To those who know me, who reach in and pull out a yes from my soul. That when I am with them my smile lingers just a bit longer in wonder and peace. To David Dixon whose own poetic artistry, sharing many poems over many days regarding the Holy Scriptures helped in this creation…and he answered yes, to all my questions.

I wonder, if you found
an empty and broken
wood snail shell
would you know it was me?
the mother of pearl sheen
still clinging within?

I wonder, would you then
pick me up, wash off the debris
lumps of mud pie, crumbling
and sticky
would you then set me down
by your pen?

Write me alive again?
take me in your hands
dry me off, satisfied
hold me up to the light
feel our longevity, resistance
feel the earth I once left

trails across forming soil
soft in your hands, molecules
adhering to one another
when they can seeking
form, divine mind making
contact with you once again.

Preface

> *I walk with only one soul, it's not mine*
> — Jenny Bates, *Fireworks*

The Choice is Always Yours

I wish I could show you
the morning of it
half-moon rise
after holding you through
the night
I showed you, last night
how it sings — its Owl voice
and Coyote tune
goose-bump-sweet and crisp.
So, I would have you step
into morning, this morning
after we held each other's
hands, each other's breath
Bluebird words — cricket
elixir you could taste them,
as I do.
Step into my Kingdom and
rise with dawn.

Table of Contents

PART I

The Choice is Always Yours..................7
Unbroken Taper..........................15
Turning Invisible........................16
Evening................................18
Take Good Notes........................20
Deluge.................................22
Everything is Equal......................24
And When You Come.....................25
Before I was born........................26
No Ordinary Passageway..................28
This is Creation.........................29
Descent to Earth........................31
Sidereal................................33
From Soil and Soul......................34
Lesson Number One.....................35
You know where I live...................37
Are you ready?..........................39
Never Cease To Be Impossible............41
Your answer............................42
plus ça change, plus c'est la même chose....44
Waiting, for............................45
Rest in peace Song of Solomon.............47
Jacob Marley's Ghost....................48
Did you get my message?.................49
Yearning...............................51
Vesica Piscis...........................53
Fear...................................55
Commemoration........................56
The Rest of the Words...................57
The Thing About Angels..................58
Just a glance will do for meditation on you....60

One Will Do 62
The Healing 63
The night I met due North. 64
Gethsemane's Ecology. 65

PART II
This is not about you and if you ask well it is 68
Divinity of Nature. 70
In to the Light 71
Those Moments. 72
Devotion. 74
Sign of the Cross 75
In the sign of fishes 77
Taking the Veil. 79
Agony 80
The Last Supper 82
At Every Station a still small voice 84
It always rains on Good Friday 86
Love in the time of Resurrection. 88
Casting First Light 90
Kyrie eleison. 91
The Source. 92
Long Enough 93
Afterword. 95
If My Prayer. 96
Canonical Hours of the Forest 97
Acknowledgments. 100
About The Author 101
In Praise of the Author. 102

*How little people know who think that holiness is dull...
When one meets the real thing, it's irresistible.*

— C. S. Lewis

When spirits come in the forest something happens first. It gets quiet. You get about ten minutes of acute, padded stillness. It's not like any other kind of stillness, any other kind of quiet, any other kind of atmosphere. This is your moment to run, if you still have the legs underneath you. Otherwise, the assumption is, you're in.

— Martin Shaw

Unbroken Taper
    or when the Forest dreams of Heaven

You can't fool me, Poetry.

even though you are my breath of prayer, and I
in my usual way sit dumb in front of you.

Say it again, you urge from the page.

I've soaked it overnight already, I reply. I can't
write sex and carnival all the time, I sigh.

St. Francis broke in the end, remember? and I
have no light to code into meaning today.

*Passion and magic, you say — hollow them out,
enchant them.*

I smell roses from nowhere, it is fifteen degrees
outside.

*Make scents to you though, doesn't it? You
could say you have written yourself.*

I could say — as I strike the match

Blessed Be.

Turning Invisible

Iwroteapoemonce
abouttalkingwithtrees
andhow/Iagreed/God/
reallywas
aLionsingingeverything
intoexistence/ormaybe
anAardvark/attheendof
hisDig/Hewouldjustkeep
diggingusoutofexistence
soHecouldgetpeaceand
quiet/somesleepinfact
Lions/enjoyadeeproar
thesoundoftheirvoice
Aardvarks/
agooddarkHole/
ButrealllyIthinkGod/
afterherested/because

later
He got arrested for
coming back to the scene

justwantedtoworkonturning
invisible/soHis/postureHis/
songisthesignal/thepattern/
the/reticulatedskinofusall/
eachdaycallinguslikea
ScandinavianKulning/the
cows/aGoodbyeofriffling
musictohaunt/anddisorder/
ourorder/Sadbecauseofits
beautyandfitsofkeening/
catharsisMaybe?I'm/making

thisup/butifyoutravelthrough
woundsandwonders/with
nospacesbetween/you'll
begintolisten/thatfaintwhistle
inyourbonesImean/
OhCrap!andtheFlood/
ofseeingandhearing
thatliltingtune/notwithyoureyes
andears/butpiercingyourblood

Evening

What a beauty you must have been
all aglow — after that dud of design
when God had the first go

like full moonlight you're born
golden locks to your feet
leaving Adam to ponder and
bleed within

he recovered it seems as he
would give you a smile only
the first Man alive could give

things had to change though
as you both got bored of gazing
and wondering where the
furniture was stored

and there was that Tree that
could not be ignored

It had not been growing and all
else was green, so Eve one night
gave it a hug — skin-tight

and to her delight it fruited
sprouting more and more buds
that bloomed —
so how could there be this sense
of doom?
Eve nurtured and spoke to both
Adam and Tree until it spoke back
— not Adam of course, the Tree

*You've healed me Eve with your
prostitute hands, so I'll teach you
the gift of Truth, it said*

*God won't like it and I'm not
sure why, but He's never around
sings to things with wings that
hang out in the sky*

*So let us begin! Go ahead eat my
Figs I'm not shy like that guy
you see, I'll share my meal
tell you everything I know*

*how ravishing you are
how to make your seeds grow*

*but pain is the price and loss
only to gain because I'll be
cut down and you will remain.*

Take Good Notes

And Into The Forest I Go To Lose My Mind and Find My Soul

                                                    - John Muir

Sometimes
I'm a neglected child
in a Russian orphanage
rocking back and forth

no one touches me

Other times
I'm an ancient oracle
who has to stay drunk
all the time on wine
or smoke

with only a spirit of
some kind to hold
me close

really nothing there
this day I do not know
the source of my soul

So
I take a break from
plowing

sort my bottles
from cardboard

Some lessons
hit rather hard
and some are
repeated

go deeper
into the woods
soul says

So I wrestle
an angel who
won't give me
his name
and laugh with
a cow or maybe
a horse standing
nearby

go deeper
into the woods
by and by

Until my steps
are strong
without privation

placed in the first place
of loving and Creation

Until I write this down:

do what we all must do
if, in the end, we too are
to become true

Deluge

Every loss begins with the Flood
the drowning of the unchosen
God and the elements making
one hell of a point

that was millennia or more ago
since then there has been many
world-shaking disasters, plagues
to cull both human and other
fellow animals

being Animals all of us might
need more training by God
and there being no corner of
the globe that escapes modern
industrial humanity's deeds
its misdeeds

So how did God choose and
really was it from greed in
the end who lived and who
sank into the face of the earth?

the Orangutan still defending his
bit of forest from bulldozers
even now we keep being asked
to grasp on to the highest point

to begin over again? like Doré's
Tigress holding her cubs her
life on the tip of a mountain
human men, women, children
clambering out of the water
beside her

She holds one cub up in her mouth
stuffed with prayer as a gift a plea
a sacrifice to an enormous distance
beyond the bounds of possibility.

Everything is Equal

Don't look back I tell myself every night
not like Lot and his wife I mean it has no
structure
this moving forward now that I set my foot
on a long path before me that may just be
mist
just keep going don't look back or in-between
if there's dry land or swelling sea chaos
reigns
or you find your way easily after the raid
of place or timing you carry a corpse
a shadow when there are no
shadows
upon your back and similarly
find the importance of unity and joy in the
journey.

And When You Come

You smell sweet and fascinating I say to the air

I've seen that God-face before

but now at this stage

I want to feel your heartbeat

hurl myself into it

until it is deafening

but what if it sounds like a lost animal

homeless — even though you never

spoke that word

Let's toast the Moon then shall we?

even though we both have thoughts

we cannot bear

I'm hungry like a tree! how about you?

I shake beside myself

hoping I still have sadness at least

Someone, not you God-face

said they knew I understood

their suffering because they could

see it in me —

don't want to become blank

still have a pattern

a shape

a beating heart to sprinkle

in your moonlit embrace.

Before I was born

I

I hear you have issues with Lions?
Let's talk then, she said

What shall I be today
your mother, your mistress
a rich whore bringing
you garlands gay or maybe the
the poor whore that makes you beg?

I've become quite a good therapist
laying naked in bed.

What's your strength Samson?
Delilah crooned and moaned

II

Samson swiveled and swerved
swooning to explain then gave in
to all that remained
All I know as I'm made!
It's my hair he said.

Your strength is my weakness
Lion slayer she said
if you lay with me now
I'll wrap myself in it
as after a bath to relax.
Samson succumbed to her soft
sheering voice and to her looks
dress and lips
and her face so fair.

III

She wrote alphabet sigils
on his bare broad body
from an angel's script Delilah traced

She was paid quite handsomely
to bring him in even though
she felt love — at least with his
skin.

IV

What angelic alphabet did
she write one wonders
as the pillars came down
together they died a panacea
from God?

We are what we think perhaps
and for me, I'm born only an idea.

No Ordinary Passageway

The Lion's eyes were like two
deep yellow pools of pollen

the Donkey beside him did not shift
though it had a faint ridge line of pulse

you could follow like clouds skirting
a mountain top

there was no wind
no curb to step down from

only the Lion, its eyes and a
dead prophet in the road

the Lion sat like a wall speaking
silently but powerfully of things unseen

Test me, it said and its eyes became
severe, yet serene

not a foot of dirt moved

By all means! spoke the Lion
at last

and the prophet was laid then taken
away on the Donkey's back

the Lion still sits on that mount
to this day

if you believe this is possible
with no memory of moving

it sits and it prays, a vigil
with the physiology of angels

for all prophets and strays.

This is Creation

I'm pondering here
but why exactly are
we bringing food to
Elijah?
Is it because
when Noah sent
us out of the Ark
first, knowing how
clever we are above
all other creatures —
especially seed eaters
we did not return
thinking Noah would
be smart enough in
return to realize we
had found land for
him and everyone left
and that of course we
would be thirsty so —
when we found that
jar stuck in the mud
a long jar well, it took
time of course to gather
and drop every pebble
we could find, takes time
you know so the water could
rise up enough for a drink
I mean! then old Noah
became impatient — and
he did not get the message
so out went the Dove and
the seed eater becomes the
hero and makes history.
Go figure.

Anyway, I'm not complaining
but this prophet is alright
doesn't complain tries
to talk to us Oh man!
but for how long as on
and on he goes hiding
from something no one
wants to explain to the Raven
thinks he can teach us to speak
even though we already
know and it is them that
forgot the words…
and Man thinks we are confusing!
Just look at how if you really
look at how we reflect in
our blackness
deep, rich and shiny!
everything mingles until
it is drawn forth out
into the light
still, it would be nice
if he kept in touch after
he leaves hey! maybe
we can teach him some of our
magic yes, that's it! about
bringing forth light —
so with each trip he makes
into darkness he will bring
more light out why didn't I
think of this before?

This is Creation.

Descent to Earth

I would hold you longer than
I probably should

so, I'll balance you like a narrow
blade
slow my fingertip along your edge

or maybe like a drop out-of-nowhere
in the air

or a shining star.

A word, that's it, one word
        the word — no

before word

because you are story inside
and out

and you fold and unfold like
that blade being forged

in fire, in water
power to do, to undo.

Come in I say then, go out

I hear your rootless laughter

as I lose my speech in your
presence
my holy words
formed in fire and water

my father, my mother.

What to say about you? to you
shaped like a blade

Love or no love shapes all things
pain or longing vulnerable
at your tip

slight movement pops and
crackles leaning in

swallowing the dialogue
of my limbs

sparks of light
compassion your grip.

Sidereal

Serious? not even a long horned beetle
can suffer my company today

resplendent am I in self-pity
poor picture of God's perfection

that's what it's all about is it not?
how we perceive ourselves every moment?

big task and some days I'm just exhausted
from it

I wish I had a photograph of my brain
at the moment of birth

and one of the night sky then too —
would they match?

does the sky remember me like the earth
remembers Jesus of Nazareth or Christ?

aren't the same thing you know, but that is
for future discussion…

well, clearly I'm not getting through to
that beetle

maybe if I hum Chopin or Debussy for him
when next we meet

probably won't be a next time though
both of us under the influence of

THE ENTIRE COSMOS
ALL OF THE TIME

pity, I would have enjoyed a new friend.

From Soil and Soul

When all is said and done, we must shut the door, get into the secret place with God, and discover what an abiding relationship with Christ will look like for ourselves.
— Bob Sorge

I have a heart of soil, a soul of creatureliness that
still wants to grow old with you

sit on a porch and chatter like birds or maybe
tree roots in the dark earth touching

just barely and blind, a core and conversation
on not knowing everything

why should we? why can't we honor the
invisible and hidden a last bastion

unusual with the beauty of language not
hunted as a carnivore competing for

nothing but a meal, a gentle tide of deepest
worship

I have a heart of soil, a soul of creatureliness
that still beats fast like lightning

roars and mumbles like thunder who we
both understand more intimately

than our own minds, minds that remain
reticent like the hunted until at last

even as it is revealed, it dies away.

Lesson Number One

One Day I found myself perched between two Black Vultures

Don't Move
and Don't Talk, said the Vulture to my left

I'll call him, Prometheus.

But!? I gulped

No argument, he hissed

The Vulture to my right, I'll call Hercules
levitated a bit from the branch we sat on

So Still, I Became.

Waiting for the Dead, I noticed the pair
of Vultures were quite clean
I wanted to let them know how lovely
they seemed,
then I remembered:

> *Don't Move*
> *Don't Talk*

I sighed and shifted until out it came…

It could be a friend of mine!

You friends with Death? Hercules chuckled

Vulture laughter sounds a bit like someone
peeing on your foot

The Shadow Committee arrived, all here
for the Wake, I shrunk down a bit
Vultures are big!

Prometheus barked in my direction,
Come if you like or sit alone
We do not serve you

I'm good, I smiled
thankful for my fast

Hercules laughed again
and I swear my foot was wet!

Be Still like God, eh? Prometheus
continued

This time, I saw him smile through his eyes.

Your love is not gone but transformed
through our Kettle

As we soar so does their soul
We are guardians now

But!? I began again

Grace serves now, Prometheus
spoke as he glided down

I looked at Hercules, he was
peeing on my other foot.

You know where I live

— There is but one freedom, to put oneself right with death. After that everything is possible. I cannot force you to believe in God. Believing in God amounts to coming to terms with death. When you have accepted death, the problem of God will be solved —and not the reverse.

—Albert Camus

I'm watching
a lone
Hummingbird
as delicate
yet strong
as the
branch it
clings to
swaying in a
playful wind

Its forays to
the feeder
are like
a carnival ride
I watch this
tiny bird
seemingly
move in
all directions
at once

flashing its
ruby throat
in angled light
it makes me
extraordinarily
quiet

like being
given
the choice
of life
or death
I think
I'm vulnerable
as the bird
I'm describing
clenching
instead of
embracing
the edge

but there are
no edges
when you
ride the wind.

Are you ready?

> *but David remained…*

Draw to me those
whom I might love
and who might love me
in return

gentle, you are like soothing oil
in my bath

this bowl of water washes me
your hands my toweling

I am a door
a threshold
a limit

I am fierce — not wild or
uncontrolled withal the
warmth of a summer's day

a lazy afternoon

my surface holds no weakness
no need
I like dancing
and bat friendly evening skies

What about you, God's own heart?
with a voice like music
that stirs the womb
fills it with Kings

you join the world together
from your balcony
and every eye seeks you

I am but a beautiful necessity
cool green grass beneath your feet

open my door? naked and unafraid
I bathe in light dried by your soul

I give you concord from sea foam
persuasion from a turquoise sea

commune with me for awhile
we'll sing a hymn of grace

under a gaze of peace.

Never Cease To Be Impossible

Before the wind comes
under my left hand
or my right
at least for a long while
I will simply bend
and be aware of you
less likely to fail that way
before the wind comes

Before the day comes
I will do something
before its too late
at least for now or ever
I shall wait stored in you
less likely to reach the
odd lucky beggar that way
before the day comes

Before the night comes
I'll skin pale fakery
elucidate passion less likely
into a sense of its worth
and need to endure light
my soul lamp flourishing
before coining the Lion's share
before the night comes

Before the wind changes
I'll break my back my breast
abreast to shift the world
with private inexorable song
less likely to strip away just like
you say alignments lost to hint
before I bring peace at last
before you come.

Your answer

We have a place now
you said to me in that

graveyard and we laughed
and cried in loneliness

I stirred you from slumber
as the earth whispers to fields

and forest then,
I summoned you back to answer

your eyes shifting like clouds
against a blue green sky

more beautiful than I remembered
symbols of wisdom

ripe on a tree
falling to my heart

asking me, Just who do you want
to be?

Time stopped as Crows gathered
curious in the trees

not many sit, talk and remember
here

they watched as if we were
a single raindrop running slowly

down a pane of glass
all the way to the bottom
at last, when I may have not answered
after all what you wanted to hear

when I realized I never got to ask
the question somewhere

deep inside my beehive tomb
a crescendo of silence then all

was your voice saying
softly *we have a place now...*

plus ça change, plus c'est la même chose

G o d

must be like a secret lover
who says one word to you
and you don't even pack
you don't look back either

you may cry *WHAT!?*

to your obsession with
this w o r d then twenty
years in you realize all you
still have is that —

s t i l l word

and you laugh and you
weep you wonder what
you are made of because
you only have that damn

one word that breaks soft
as cobweb silk wrapped
in eider and green moss
at twilight that breaks again

like a fern in shade —
then and again he comes
to help you gather some
words to grind in your

sleep asleep he scatters
you up with only
one word that does not
begin with I Am…

Waiting, for

A good friend and his new wife
visiting from LA yesterday says,
through hearing stories and laughter
and tears,

You don't live with Wildlife, you live
with Life

I thought God has unparalleled
expression and G o d is trying
so hard to help us through the
waiting
he gives us gift after gift and we
become numb

a poet can have a quicksilver tongue
a charm to migrate snakes and
butterflies

yet still sit and wait standing alone
for a perfect time that never comes
to command her way and witty
repartee

faux-extroversion so it seems and
I am bathed in smoke once again
Venusian, Mercurial tongue-tied
to extremes

prayers erecting a honey pot for
sigils and the warm bosoms of bees.
Standalone I wait in-between
Unicorn feet and piercing horn
a sacrifice for me

as I say to my friend and his wife
from LA
their rented Tesla singing as it backs
away
listen closely…you can hear the trees
reap with cloud, sow with wind.

Rest in peace Song of Solomon

Love consists in this, that two solitudes protect and touch and greet each other
— Rilke

Whatever is asked of me I said to the song
the words in this song
I know it by heart by its smell of sweet musk
and all of the forest

it roams

by my unbroken sleep that prolongs my life
or is it my death?

I shall not conceal it in shadow or cloud

I shall not conceal it after the flood after
the night
when youth no longer exists

Why should I?

I am not the same girl who promised or
promises

I have my spear
I have my grave

I am a hundred women bearing no wealth
or weapon

I offer anyway

not thinking to do you harm but to touch
the least part of you
your flesh squinters at my fingertips
as I draw your Light

from thirsty dark letters.

Jacob Marley's Ghost

The most difficult part of candle magic
is making yourself burn the candle
when you should

I healed a Dog once

a good friend called me up in a panic
said her nine year old Saint Bernard
Jacob Marley

got bit by a snake in her yard
and the whole of his back leg
was swollen

she did not call the vet, she called me

she said she lit every candle full of
prayer inside and out and she called
me, said I could save him

I did too

It took from morning till dusk
to press and soothe and speak
and oh so many hot compresses

but the puss finally came

and when I left Jacob Marley,
the last time I ever saw him
he was standing

wagging his tail and my good
friend was crying all the way
to getting him his dinner.

Did you get my message?

After you unpacked me
my scent
my aesthetic
my spiritual
material
character

all those forged connections
we make over
days
nights
hours
calculated
managed
folded
tucked
like a sheet

did my communication
stain
or flame
you?
burn like embers
unattended
kept
out of reach
or do
you wear it directly
on your worn body?

a balm from Asclepius
or the heart
of a
Lion say —

always
mindful
that it is full
of
holes
and jagged edges

the shadow of a Dragonfly
landing
on
your shoulder
for only
a
brief
moment —
then gone

God is so kind
or
so
we
hope
walking that
uneven
shoreline
with us.

Yearning

*You could say one word
I could retract my claws
though they have great
purpose
serve me well
I could lay at your feet
like a house
cat
so then, what will this
word be, Daniel?*

Daniel breathed.

*What syllable or
symbols before your
angel arrives?
we'll be forgotten
then down in this pit
stinking and starving
after your're gone they'll
throw us a Lamb*

*I am a King! but no
Judah you see
I suffer each moment
and you see what
what you see
is left of my family*

Daniel listened all night
wept with the stars
silent and sorrowful
he dreamed with this
King of the Desert
even danced with Him

Morning rose like a
rabbi though no light
reached the den
there at his feet lay the
hungry lion King

so before any angel
could intervene Daniel
lay his hand on each head
each golden mane shone
for a moment as he
prayed yearning for
their freedom
deliverance for all
an angel looked on
and spoke the word,

Mercy.

Vesica Piscis

Write the wrongs that are done to you in sand, but write the good things that happen to you on a piece of marble...
—Arabic Proverb

It was the beating

three days now

that sonic driving

of the drum

I've sang, I've danced

to its frame, its drub

somewhere deep inside

this body

I know I must leave

to become myself

but what if you

don't like me?

Listen! my dream

you told me this

must be done

Listen! my body

you said this

should be the way

Don't lie to me

my feet as I run

toward these giant

pearl gates

to these teeth

I speak I pray

and find myself

ashore

outlived by grace.

Fear

A Deer steps out in the trees and stops

directly in front of you

You stop and look at the Deer

You become the Deer

You can do it, you tell yourself

Then, you hear the snap of a twig

a snort of warning and you bolt

You run, graceful yes, but you run.

Commemoration

Memories roost like Vultures
in their favorite tree

it's a delightful tradition

I reached for my old study Bible
from college and the spine

tore away
don't worry, I said

you still care for my soul

somewhere in there
I have loved you too

though I can't say I ever
liked you much

kind of like the new King
of England who got

crowned this morning
everyone really preferring his son

my memory of You is too moral
and alone

calling us like the Bobwhite
whose returning to our woods

we are glad to hear him back
but his call is never answered

the Royal Horses were beautiful
in the coronation parade
hell, even I would have stepped
in their poop without flinching.

The Rest of the Words

*The fishes that swim — the rocks the motion of the waves —
what stranger miracles are there?*
                              —Walt Whitman

It would have been hard to be
a scribe to a prophet

write down everything they say
every minute of the day

like a river that hooks you
into transcendent information

don't know where it comes from
only how it comes

surrounded by light crashing
over its banks

with total conviction

fear it?
yes

desire it?
most certainly

is it Real? well, if it
passes this test

act upon it
even if
no one believes you.

The Thing About Angels

There's a divinity that shares our ends, rough-hew them how we will
— William Shakespeare Hamlet, V. ii

You can turn over a stone and start
their celestial fluttering
that's usually how they speak
between vaporous pinions or
maybe heartbeats

Oh there is a hierarchy no doubt
but they're team players and they
don't just intervene in human
affairs either
they are up to saving animals
when it suits them, remember
Balaam's Donkey?
I'm betting you do

And they're mute sometimes —
not announcing like the three to
Abraham and a few more I
could think of

They aren't always Light —
more clothed in darkness
like a star
Why I saw one once sitting on
a branch as a Squirrel staring
into my room until I gave in to
joy not doom
I like sitting with the dumb —
what some would call animals
because there is just no small talk
either silence or all in voices
like those Old Testament angels

They said what they had to then they
left — just like a wild creature or
our furry four footed friends have
done and will do, long before we
want them to

Angels don't stick around
usually leave like a shadow
in the day — you think
I'm contradicting myself
when I say that but next time
the night comes and moonlit
rocks begin glistening

If you listen you may hear
a cry or a bark as you hush
your sophisticated fear
see light move slowly across
your eyelids shut tight and
feel the assembling the
trembling of wings.

Just a glance will do for meditation on you

You know who you are

the love that nibbles

on your ear

not making sense to

anyone else

did you hear me then

or now?

My mother would

tell the story, when

I was five I saw an

angel sitting at her

sewing machine

glowing white

against Singer green

with wings and a

face I later found

in Leonardo's notebooks.

My mother said it

was my soul sitting

there guarding its

creation.

Dove light, she said

like that seen at the

river Jordan, I suppose.

My soul smiled, I remember

like a spiritual stream

disappearing down a hill.

I'm just matter, and lots

of it

I can drink Glow tea

to quarantine grief

but I'll depart from a stage

less tragic than say

a beetle.

I am a stone

not a pearl

only able to weave

this idea of sewing

into a poem.

One Will Do

There are many angels out there

not all white pressing spirits

some, press us down to

the frost bitten earth

some are heavy

to keep you warm when you

are so cold

       so cold
       so cold

some don't fall from the sky

but come up from the wild earth

not to crush us

to lift us up

one may be plenty though

only a breath apart

looking deep into your eyes

touching your heart

like a waterfall singing

in the distance.

The Healing

When you look at your hands and feel
suddenly the great age of the place

you've lived in and you try, really try
to detach from this landscape leaving

a long gap as you would like between
each line you see reading what lines

on your hands still remaining
close your eyes and breathe

and your intuition says it's a gift
and your understanding says it's a rift

and your expectations say it's your core
but your thinking says you've switched off

your hands where extra places are laid
to feed the not the living but the dead

you try again looking for all the world
like your praying under the most beautiful

tree with the most beautiful hands like feathers
that you have ever seen.

The night I met due North

My name is Heavenly, said the Bear
in tones of dark deep matter.

There he lounged lazily bound atop
the crescent Moon.

*A green comet touched the top of my tail
one I had not seen for a little while.*

*Has it been that long? Fifty thousand years?
Oh dear, how time flies!*

*Mary, Mother of the Christ lets me lay here
in her lap. She strokes my ears, says she*

*misses her son. Protects me from the arrows
of Sagittarius, Hercules, and Orion's Crux
and club.*

*She knows I miss my mother, but a secret
I'll reveal to you.*

*I'm really guarding the Golden Apples that
make all dreams come true.*

*Mary and I we are writing a new Gospel
one where sky meets earth.*

*We've talked to the Pleiades and Nazca lines
and they want to contribute too.*

*The central plane we put this down on is of course
the Milky Way.*
Would you sing me a lullaby? Heavenly finally asked
*just as Sirius recedes? He is quite a good dog, but
he is so bright, I haven't quite caught up to speed.*

Forgive me, he continued on, *I forgot to ask your
name?*

Gethsemane's Ecology

Instead, I reasoned with God, telling him to bring the fox back because he deserved a longer life. Did I believe that God would answer my prayer? Yes, I knew he would. Not because I believe in God, but because I knew that God believed in foxes.
— Catherine Raven

Can you show me how it's done? falling in love with that
invisible God and His Son.

A thorny business, in limited space.
Horse nettle existence, like an undesirable but attractive
weed.

And Who's to say it is the Fox, not I, that He had in mind
to multiply?

Somehow, certain words, those Paradise terms,
grew taller than others — mixing everything up!

So now only perennial and deep plowing will help
eradication and crying.

You can touch a Fox with a single whiff, you will never
forget
his psalm, the balm of looking into his eyes.

Without worship, without respect, without wonder, without the great work with which our wonder and awe plunge us, what is there — what?

— Alfred Kazin

This is not about you and if you ask well it is

none of your damn business

and you want to travel with Him,
and you want to travel blind and then you
think maybe you'll trust Him For He's touched
your perfect body with His mind...
— Leonard Cohen

I hope not to be afraid

of the rain
of the smile
of the wind
of the time
of the nakedness
of the leaving
of the taking
of the tie taken out of my
hair letting it down without
care for its stripes of grey
and white
its slight...irregularities

I hope not to be afraid

of your hands
of your touch
of your memory
of your gaze
of a tone
of a sound
of a boon
of a shroud

you said you love to sit
in silence but don't want
to be alone that it's your
second home
a porch
with that dog at your feet
with me at your feet
that dog full of light not
darkness so you won't be afraid

of the rain
of the smile
of the wind
of the time
of the memory
of my nakedness
of my hands
of my touch
of my gaze
of my peace
as I wash your perfect body
with my hair.

Divinity of Nature

If you lose something
you have not wholly understood

Nothing is Holy.
I would shade you under the most

beautiful tree ever made.
Then, I would dapple you

with sunshine as you listen,
the peace of the vast Forest

I would serve to you with clove,
star aniseed, willow bark, orange.

Let the breeze lift you to a high place
as you breathe in its fire

on your skin, its water
at your feet.

Guide you back to where you began.
As I let you go like a leaf on the wind.

In to the Light

My loneliness writes to you now
just like all the other John Does
so I'll take these words consecrate
them alone
Your light ascending descending
is all the same otherwise I'm sure
I could not do or speak but with an
expressionless face

I knew a thousand pound Bull once
who laughed and peed when I read
poems to him in the field
There she is again, he'd croon to
a friend, I hope it's brief today

If I am a vessel than the earth
is a bowl a grail of stone for
both I and that Bull to linger
to bathe in?

Being a misfit a nothing is hard
to get used to like drinking snow
water for tea, if there is any snow

Wreathed in a garland of tiny birds
we got along very well together
I and that Bull in that field of
patience and truth

Did you in your light really mean
to free us?

Those Moments

Think about it, being you

everything, everyone you touched
or touched you

you became

sensory overload twenty-four-seven

even cloth — cloth! absorbed your
image

didn't you leave something else
almost human behind?

hair, nails, a childhood toy,
a doodle?

oh, ok I and everyone else you left
here makes up our own

version of you

I get the all around presence
filling eyes and love

everywhere

but...my apologies
this can be a distraction

so I look at this tree
in front of me

and it leaves me wondering
just how do you see the green?
my question a selfish plea
for space in your head

like a breeze softly floating
across your face

I see your hair rising
and falling

stroke my hand in it
I glance into your eyes

and you are there
simply by my side.

Devotion

Still water carves you up

you think you're umbelliferous

a clove whose smell being the essence of

Christmas is your umbrella

your oils held just beneath the surface

oh you may not be the loudest voice

in the choir

but you are sweet

you can lace your ardor up like a shoe

but your chances still sound like the

twirl of cotton candy.

Sign of the Cross

Lo, I am with you always,
he said

and I believe him
oh not the Throne of God

stuff, who would want all
the noise and glory

and how could you hear
your own soul think

let alone someone who
says he's

always with you

I want the Christ dethroned
and sandaled

barefoot even better
who knows how the tip

of a wheat stalk feels
or what the leaves laugh

about in the wind

someone to cry for my dogs
and the donkey he left behind

forever marked by his cross

someone who's really
accomplished

yet might prefer
the plain and undone

I walk a path almost every day
to see an old friend

I know is not there
she won't run up

to greet me but I walk
this path anyway

talk the same way
we always did

that's what I want
from someone who says

'till the end of time

so I can speak to
and be spoken to

by the stars.

In the sign of fishes

If the spirit is the true self
as Cicero claimed
then I hope mine is as playful
as an Otter
though I would like to know
its name

Some say that certain stones
hold the prayer
certain stones hold the answer
if so, I would like to ask
how hidden can one be!?

and what does the breath of God
sound like, seems to me
he doesn't talk very often by
anyones recollection

we may live by words written
in a book, but God quit writing
long ago and it is touch and
sometimes not even that,
that heals us

The first time I heard the air
becoming the breath of a
Lungfish — *who like the soul*
lives in two worlds, neither
built for land or sea

begging the question what is he?

I thought it the most beautiful
sound I ever heard
so I would rather hear God breathe.

Judas in his Gospel said the spirit
lives in a place where
no angel has ever seen
no thought of the heart has
ever comprehended
and it was never called by any name

I'm ok with this
God needs his own private space
but when he gets to feeling like
a lonely champion
he reaches out with a shadow,
a fingertip, a breath in your face

and you gasp and engage as that
Lungfish at nothing and everything
becoming beautiful again.

Taking the Veil

If I get too close to you
I'd have to become a nun
asleep in lineage undone
not hillwalking future

yet St. Clare stayed awake
I tell my aging lines
she told stories and lived
them with her love, St. Francis

now don't get yourself
in a bind here though
their love fused strong

more like if you were really
good at cooking, fly-fishing
poetry or woodworking

someone to gleam the grace
of evening with
keep the sea or firelight going

because in your garden —
and yes, that one too
Mary's lap already held her
shrouded Son

earthly and spiritual delights
are the same as prayers in
Gethsemane

waves of smoke over your
heart
living flames from sleeping
embers
never covered over.

Agony

I would have perhaps danced into my future
like the Grouse,
knowing what is to come

or maybe taken flight like restless Doves,
the soul always wanting to be green
and growing

but Christ you stayed, so I tend to think
I should do the same

even though I don't want to be the one
that can't let go.

In Spain there was a day townsfolk
took drunk to the streets

a live Donkey was crowned with a
dunce cap and dragged

pummeled by filth, hit with sticks
shouted and puked upon

mangled and broke

just like a walk through with a Cross
that Jesus took.

I've never understood.

I'm glad He got angry at least once
in his life.

That town in Spain uses an effigy now
or maybe they've stopped
though I can't see how, because
every year

we celebrate death so I still have a
question

would I rise to the call if it were
me instead?

The Last Supper

you can't fool an animal
they know when it is
their last meal

I mean look at me!
stuttered Coyote
as he broke
another piece
of himself and
the bread

passed it on to others
instead

*I would serve each one
but…*

*But you can't save them
all, least of all
the least*
Pharisee said

as they both watched
Coyote's grave being dug
it's a good day to die
they heard someone cry

*The world or my word
is a dream built upon
dreams
all of us from the tiniest
amoeba to Blue Whale,*
Coyote shook spilling
his wine, his blood

I doubt it, said Thomas

*Do not lose your patience
with me,* spoke Coyote
who struggled to keep
his eyes on the others

not his hands or his feet

*I'll always be hunted
but I'll never be the same
remember the flowers?
each in its own form and
anyway, all things change*

Teach us again, said Peter

Coyote let out a sigh, then
he began with, *I'll try*

*Not all things are taught
and the oldest of languages
cannot be bought*

gently Coyote looked
up at his friend

*You were supposed to teach
us everything!* cried out Judas
at last

Well, said smiling Coyote
*if you want to know all
you must go ask a Mouse.*

At Every Station a still small voice

Keep looking at me
and I'll keep walking
I whisper to the Bird
dying in my hands —
today of all days
I have a pebble
in my shoe but I
leave it there as
I condemn this little
Bird to death and
what of the Bear
sighted at the edge
of the road yesterday
coming out of the
woods?
That pebble is painful
and I fall almost
thinking I can save
this Bird if I only
keep walking
and whispering
Where is your mother?
I ask I would like
to meet her
I find help at last
a dandelion full
of sun
I wipe the Bird's
face its head falls
forward I weep
because women
weep
The Bird falls

forward again
I strip and wipe
it's beak free of
pollen thinking
to help it
breathe again
it can't breathe
I cry again
I nail my soul
to its soul that
Bear as well
even though he
was in no trouble
at all
I walk the Bird
down the road
to the Rock I go
back and pick
the dandelion
place the Bird's
head on it gently
I sit on the Rock
and wait
I forget about the
pebble in my
shoe until now
when it wakes
and tells me to
become the pebble

It always rains on Good Friday

Mary

If I lie quietly a few moments
I could carry you like a prayer

my arms instead of arms ending
in hands — brightly colored birds

to free your body softly thinking
of a destination

and I could be there
but I can't

so I hold you as you shoot up
to the clouds toward the moon

I'm here with this earth coming
to a close

with your body coming
to a close.

Magdalene

I'm a chaotic being uttering
prayers and blessings

of love at once at this Stone
my tears that hold you now

no house, no temple, not even
a grave, my song

no heavenly choir but a deep
call from a whale

my lilac bushes are gone
but there you are in front of me

a bee creating honey from
flowers of the moon

bright colored flowers hot
with light as the world
becomes your charity

blowing open in a gentle
breeze

teach me how to hear
you now

to open my memory to carry
the history of us all.

Love in the time of Resurrection

When I remember your love I weep...
something in my chest, where nothing much happens
now, moves as in sleep
                                                    — Rumi

Trees remember

just cut one open and see

when they cut me open

I felt pain

but not like you

I'll try to explain

when they nailed you to me

your blood and my veins

merging over and over again

you leaned into me

allowing me to work

to accept what it was

what it is

is:

medicine

my breath became yours

as you bled against

my thighs

my arms

my hands

you cried and I let you

my rings of memory

became your crown

your thorns my nails

my holy grail weighing

two hearts beating

obediently down

so when we touch

each other now

we bloom.

Casting First Light

the first day of the week cometh Mary Magdalene early, when it was yet dark, unto the sepulcher… Jesus said unto her, Mary…

What

if

the

only

thing

left

of

my

heart

is

your

shadow?

Kyrie eleison

Oh holy living creatures forgive us

I say to earthworm struggling in the

rain.

Forgive us I say to the astrolabe who

calculates prayer as well as anything

can.

There are no longer open-ended rules

Probability is not the only consideration

Probably, that earthworm will get eaten

Probably prayers will get eaten like caviar

Rows of them flaked, digested by some

Gospel in the stars.

Not knowing the sacrifice on Golgotha

changed the entire earth forever.

The Source

What is the source?
and does it invite or receive
your invitation

to join in it, with it?
Would you source yourself
out to say, a dying rabbit?

is there illumination there
or
a lowering like melting snow?

We have met before on this bridge,
I say to the Wolf who eats the rabbit.

He picks up a Crow feather with his
teeth

offers it to me, does not leave me
to return across the bridge.

Bear arrives, he stays by my side
speaks of renewal, I lay my hand

on his massive head
but he turns,
lumbers back across the bridge.

Crow plucks another feather
from his tail and drops it at my
feet. Giving thanks like a cloud

crossing many landscapes
flies to my outstretched arm.
We know each other well, Crow
says.

Long Enough

Listen to the crow call when the wind stops
— Mary Ricketson

How to say this
in the end
tell it like it is —
that old phrase

a viable future for words
not their abandonment
because find becomes more
elusive than search

so if we haven't figured
God out by now
we begin again as if we
really know what to look

for in the first place
we live with the long enough
pursuit like an open wound
watch its personality emerge

like a newborn or puppy
only to pour out its spirit
what do you want to call it?
chewing away or caring

we put our face against
the wound say its nothing
and not the first time our
feet have been covered in blood.

AFTERWORD

Most of these poems were inspired by Gustave Doré's Illustrations of the Bible, both Old and New Testaments. They are in Biblical order. The rest are my musings on things in-between… I have been described as an "irredeemable aviphile." I accept irredeemable gladly, and I know of things with wings who hold prayer with each ruffle and beat.
I deliberately chose additional poems to include in the Preface, Special Thanks, and Afterword…why not? and how better to express my true self in gratitude.

If My Prayer

is the imagination of Nature
the spark of God

call it whatever you like
you better pray it's still there

prana
chi
ki
wodan
wakan
Nous

not like a noose you catch
a Rabbit with

but one that makes you see
that Rabbit has power worth

getting to know and preserve

not like in a jar, like in a cloud
a point of light
a spiral

that will penetrate
permeate
conduct
refract
absorb

a fingerprint of
shortwave
longwave
gamma ray

blended like a smoothie.

if you care
about my prayer

then put those whorls of yours
together, bend those elbows

like you're waiting on the last bus
to the other world

I'll be there my prayer
is speaking

my prayer is asking.

Canonical Hours of the Forest

Matins
Wake up! the Crow
as the crow flies…you can find your own answers
One, Two, Three caws
Jesus was a sailor but you think
you need wings to travel with Him.

Lauds
Wake up! the Snapping Turtle
Three caws again, look up I say
fateful turns, blocks in all those branches
Better groom those wings
Odysseus knew
tried to be a sailor too.

Prime
Wake up! the Fox
Three little hours to begin
Emily Dickinson believed
in possibility
yet never ventured far from her home
must not have been
hungry, hungry, hungry.

Terce
Wake up! the Coyote
Nunc Sancte nobis Spiritus
Can't walk on water?
No problem

Consider other virtues
Follow the Crow

Sext
Wake up! the Deer
Can't, already awake long before
So Jesus was born in a makeshift shelter
Look how he turned out
Crow says to the fawn born under a bush
Look, Look, Look

None
Wake up! the Mink
Somebody wrote a song about Number 9
the remains of the day
Uh oh, forgive me
Have to leave the comfort and safety of home
especially at dusk
over and over and over

Vespers
Wake up! the Opossum
Ah, evening
raft of religion
transport to dreams
I have to die now
so excuse me
but I'll remember you
if you promise to
Remember me, Remember me, Remember me

Compline
Wake up! the Tree
The great silence of Night
Do you think it's haunting?
It never sleeps by the way
only becomes a receptacle
a womb, a presence that holds you
until you don't exist

Acknowledgments

Gratitude for the publishers of these poems included in this book

Silver Birch Press, 2023: Divinity of Nature

Indelible Journal: London Arts-Based Research Centre, 2022: Fireworks [epigraph]

About The Author

Jenny Bates, five poetry books, published in numerous NC and international journals. Presented at the 2023 Ecopoetics and Environmental Aesthetics Conference, London. Jenny was a judge for the Poetry in Plain Sight contest through the NC Poetry Society, 2024. Her newest book of poems, ESSENTIAL, Redhawk Publications 2023 has been nominated for the Pushcart Prize 2024. Jenny's books are also available at Malaprops Bookstore in Asheville, NC and the Book Ferret, Winston-Salem, NC.

www.ingramcontent.com/pod-product-compliance
Lightning Source LLC
Chambersburg PA
CBHW021019090426
42738CB00007B/833